SAFE DANGER

SAFE DANGER

POEMS

STEPHEN ZERANCE

INDOLENT BOOKS

© 2018 Stephen Zerance

Author Photo: Daniel Wickerham

Cover and book design: adam b. bohannon

Book editor: Nicholas Oliver Moore

Published by Indolent Books,

an imprint of Indolent Arts Foundation, Inc.

www.indolentbooks.com

Brooklyn, New York

ISBN: 978-1-945023-14-9

CONTENTS

III.

IV.

I.

True Crime

In the home invasion, the husband meets the baseball bat. The three
    women go up
with the house. For thirty minutes the police watch, do absolutely
    nothing. Everyone

wants the outcome to be so different. The case could've been
    prevented at many turns—the rape, strangulation, pouring of
    gasoline. I've been watching true crime, still not afraid

of strangers. The killer is usually family: close, loved, known. When
    the beauty queen
was discovered bludgeoned, garroted, body on stage—the fingers all
    pointed

inside the house. I've tried to rationalize abject crime, my fascination.
    Both have always
been around. I love the idea of what is impossible for myself. When I
    pop the razor

from under my tongue and think it over—the simplest explanation—I
    revolve
around danger. Talking to strangers, a white mane grows out my
    feet—it's hard to keep

a story straight. The horses want to get loose. In the home invasion,
    the mother says

they're *nice men* to the bank teller. She returns to the rape,
    strangulation, pouring

of gasoline. The story all at once is pointless. There is a luxury of
    being alive. In my life
there's nothing wrong. I want to light it on fire. I'm a weapon with no
    safety.

4   When I enter a room I must go off.

Marsyas

The radiator's hiss catcalls me
     out the door, ribcage and pale
limbs in a tank top three sizes

too large. I'm angel of my corner bar,

Marsyas

The radiator's hiss catcalls me
    out the door, ribcage and pale
limbs in a tank top three sizes

too large. I'm angel of my corner bar,   **5**
with no problem going alone, lonely
    as I am, Stranger. I drink

until one eye is bigger than the other,
  until I talk close to you, blue and
    glass eyed. Tear me away

    from myself, through the open veins
of the city—golden and skinned alive
    into dawn, through doorway to you.

  I am knife thin, Stranger, thinner than reed
    slit between the teeth. Thinner
than pitted string on the lyre. Do

as you please tonight. I do not like
to be touched on my back, that one
wound that rings as the music—

Gay Fiction

Those books I devoured
about the abyss of love
through sex where man
ends solo, or can't come
to the party, where cancer
entertains, candles lit
then snuffed one by one,
the smoke leaves all
at the farewell symphony.
O my Satan, I've never
been so sad that sex
is still fun when sick
with slut in the hour
of nightwalkers. There
you are: a piece in everyone.
I want to die surrounded
by candy, a city
and a pillar in my mouth.
I'll wear a mask, confess
nothing but these words.
These are days to keep
the dead, to cling to
the living desire inside
not to be afraid. Caution
when consuming men:
the symptoms start

with unsteady muscle
control, wild
laughter, convulsion,
awakening in unfamiliar
surroundings unable
to stand. Welcome
to the strange room.

Hymn to Isis

Take the pill, call it drive,
the simple rhythm

played on the sistrum back and forth

for the goddess no one has seen.

What does Isis look like? Her faith
in my shaven body I prep

in the rear temple. Where is music
in stomach ache? In the dream, all was good

if excessive, as my inner workings
were on parade, colorful, loud.

The Oracle, what does she know
about excess? I'm dancing

among my minnows
in my revels against

God. I never trust a vision
that comes from inside

the earth, only the work on the body
as I recollect Osiris,

recovering his parts
from the ocean until he is created.

I remember the first time
with purification, a member

on the rocking boat daily,
finger to my lips to keep it secret.

Lindsay Lohan

Sedate in your mug-shot, I'd worry
my eyebrows weren't impeccably plucked,
my chin double.
I'd love to be unable to move my face.
Pinch my skin taut behind my ears.
Pump my lips. Pump them
to a permanent Lindsay pout.
I don't fear needles, incisions, or drills.
File my teeth down to the nub. Give me
veneers. I've got a daily ritual:
eye serums, white-strips, line breakers,
ten push-ups each time I walk into
my bedroom, crunches over crunches
over lies.
Suck my stomach to permanent morning.
Snap my nose straight.
Lindsay, I'd steal that necklace.
And I'd wear it out in public for everyone
to notice. Because it was mine. Because
if you believe so deeply that something
is yours, that it belongs to you, then it does.

Inside

my father's closet, the suits run
on wooden hangers color-coded
deep into the back, brown to navy
pinstripe to gray.

Tucked behind a black suit dust
clings to a green jacket a patch
on the arm, still bright yellow,
the cloth stiff.

oOxfords line the floor, end at a boot
where the rough laces are tucked
into tongues.

I am frightened by his rifle
from Vietnam behind the door
resting below the light switch, a still
from a movie I've never seen.

I'm afraid it will blow off my hand.

Siberia

He is driving. His hand moves to my knee.
While he chats about his life in Russia,
I stare at the red patch on his knuckle.
It's cold as Siberia, I mention.

He describes the weather in Russia
as I roll up the window, turn on the heat.
It's not that cold in Siberia—I'm corrected,
nervous that it is contagious

as he rolls up his window, cranks up the heat.
I stare at the red patch on his knuckle.
Don't worry, he says, *It's not contagious.*
He is driving. His hand is on my knee.

The Bathed One

Publicly displayed in a vat, marigolds
fumigate my eyes. I drum
my obsidian mouth. Each morning
I am washed, my skin collapses
around the sternum, free
of blemish. In my regimen

I learn to walk. One foot over
the other on stairs. I awake
in zinnia. His hands are tender,
he brings me tobacco. Hummingbirds tick.
I play a ceramic rasp, dance
and inhale violets.

My need is great. At midnight,
smoothed alabaster, I sing on a bed
of whistles until my voice is ghost,
hair matted with down. Tonight,
there is a golden tinge to objects,
my flesh keeps the soul hostage.

On the seventh morning, my captor
extracts my dahlia heart, steals it
with a flint razor. I dangle there,
severed at the wrists.
For twenty days, I am worn
inside out, then sloughed.

The Veil Always Remains

911 is down, an emergency—quick
murder someone, throw a party.
What will I wear as the host

in red blue flash? I can't even tell you
why I'm mad, spiraling as the staircase
I've wanted to throw myself down

for months. Tonight, I've no desire
to dance but I'll move for your head
on a silver charger, you say

my name, I'll have your mouth—
I haven't eaten in days. Your body
is the body I'll take

for a minute, a firefly inside
a locket. You can't hurt me—my body
is vampire fresh, better off dead

having kissed your mouth. Your body—
a scaled jewel, a mirror. You'll never
know what I believe. Will

you ever be free, one eye
on the razor, a head pierced
with swords? Music to my ears,

this infatuation curse
I spill over you, the body I need,
never needed.

Diet of the Saints

For the first time I look vulgar,
blown up muscles down my V,
I make love to myself all night

keeping the machine churning,
arm on the rack in a hair weighted
vest, beating heart, legs on the press.

Water, water, water—I'm better,
I'm the best gymnasium idol
with my cosmetic intuition. O my

poor, poor kidney, I don't know
if I'm getting closer to God or
the devil when I piss electric yellow

with my kick in the mouth: five
vita-caps, white water pill, red
for jitters—I'm falling into myself

while horses gallop down my throat.
Nothing on me by this diet of saints
with their scourges, chains, spiders,

thorns. It doesn't hurt, no—
the harvest is habit, all infinitive:
to keep at it, to stay wasting

consumptive holding the pose, to
visit the monster I've created daily.
I'm all meat, learning how to suffer.

Anne Sexton's Last Drink

I came out of the Charles River,
a sunflower smiling at you on empty soil,
rising full light in your hand out of need

to travel through the galleys
of your memory, a donkey on a crash
course—I'm the driver. You can't flee

yourself—that putty, iron maiden
of the mind that converts you back
to the witches. Any plans you had—

I made them instead. Put on
your mother's best mink for a burning.
Turn circles alone, ignite into the front
seat of your sealed loading zone.

La de da,
how does it feel when I row
the world back? You'd say—
cordial. Quite the gentleman.

Cobra

To the lord of shedding

    at seventeen: my legs. This

is how I want them: slick,

    defined, so bare the veins pop

down their sides split

    with muscle—the thought

drives me to glide

    a Bic up my calf to the thigh,

and repeat, working in the tub until

    the water is hair, until the porcelain

has a halo. I've spent an hour. I can't

    recognize my legs. I pick out

the drain, slip into pants, walk around

the house like everything

is fine, till the moment my sister

notices my ankle

20   while I lie in the living room,

smooth.

On the Casting Couch

Mr. Magic Man, I grew at midnight
with a need for consumerism,
a dramatic ritual

I'm unwilling to pay for. I'll spare details
of childhood, chalk it up
to myth. Make this easier—lop off

my midsection, slit me ear
to ear—it's easier to speak to me without a face
or clothes. There's no fear

when I'm felt up, I stumble with my mouth
and will raise Babylon
by tongue. I've whitened

my teeth, gums derelict,
in credit card debt but I love
myself, it is my only passion.

My body tells me something. A cough—
but I ignore it. What is air?
Who are you? I'm nice

and firm. I don't remember
names—that twilight language—
but know the lines.

Scary Movie Marathon
The Amityville Horror

Here is the house:
dog twisted around
pickets in the backyard,
red hot pokers the mother
plants out front, dolls
the sister lines facing the wall—
sewing room, needle work
in the halls, the father
balancing books in the basement, high
hopes. The son—
behind the staircase.
Open the doors, see
the demons. There's
Jesus upstairs in prayer.
I don't remember the belt
or wooden spoon
as the siblings are led
in drill through the house,
marching band of blame
in the light of a half-moon.
The house is aflare. The path
to my bedroom in smoke.
The occurrence is consistent.
A figure welcomes itself in.
The house is always on fire.

How To Begin

Strip your life
as Venus and Mars align,
catching you
staggered as traffic
swims the wrong way
down a one-way street.

Throw all of your gold
in a lake. Wait for it to rise
to walk you through the city
on your eyes. Change
your name. Get kicked out

of the after party
for having the wrong card,
for holding two glasses up,
three poured back.

Notice the gray in your hair.
Notice something split in your hair.

Hold two glasses up. Pour
three back at the after party
for having the wrong card.

Get kicked out. Your name—
changed. On your eyes
walk through the city
waiting to rise. In a lake,

find all the gold you need.
Walk the wrong way down
a one-way street
staggered as traffic
is caught, as Mars
and Venus align.

Strip your life
is how to begin.

Ritual

Slice me nice
where you work
down my back,
pierce my spine
into a hawk
with thirteen bronze
pins so I may
think of you.
I walk around
the neighborhood
three times
to find my lover
gone. A street
with each car's
windows bashed out
passenger side
offers me the city
I desire, the rooms
of my mind.

I come home
to find a window
open, broken into.
A man had walked
into my life,

looked around,
stole nothing—

but painted
my body turquoise,
double-headed serpent
in the throes of July,
to dart into a mouth
to lap the precious water,
to dance bewitched,
dancing mad.

After It Rains

This morning in my dreams: a dog blind
with rabies unravels my stomach

in a fenced yard I can't escape. A cockroach
inches across the ceiling, retracts its wings, drops

right in my mouth and I'm fastened
to the bed. The interpreters say these images

equate dirtiness at home, or the betrayal
of a beloved. This has nothing to do

with health. They say it's time to take off
the rose-tinted glasses. It's time to clean house.

Today after it rains—nothing but evictions
all down Park Ave—endless tables, chairs,

sofas all carelessly flooding the banks
of the sidewalks, as if Baltimore loosened itself

inside-out. As if the city regurgitated
bricks. Today, I looked down

out of the blue and noticed my fingers—
all the skin on each tip had peeled back.

I can name a million reasons.

Love Song

Yes yes I can play I love you I love you
not daisy petal game take my finger bite

off my whole arm please am I playing
with myself or you I can't tell anymore I'm

blind yes yes in a fantasy yes an infant
in a rural idyll beneath the monarch sun

butterfly sting on my eye I'm a caged jaguar
I love you love you not you say through a split

tongue yes yes you are conductor I'll stay
dormant operator I'll strum an orchestra

as you pace black-booted slicked back I've
imagined you an angel dying a natural

death yes yes in the doorway the last
petal left pulled means a certain death yes

Mosquito

Swatted four today on the wall as they danced
to waste. They know breathing.

They sense a warm body at night
from the leaves and shrubs they hide in.

The female travels to saw her mouth across skin,
to collect flesh to grow pregnant, cause

the bite on the skin, the infection, rather.
Once I was eight and fell into a nest,

wandered off the trail away from my sister,
touched the larvae hidden under ivy. All

up my arms, eruptions running through
the Blue Ridge mountains.

And what of the males?

All they do is swarm at dusk, fuck, live
a week mostly concerned with nectar.

If given a choice, even in a lab, between
blood or sugar, they will always choose sugar.

Komodo Dragon

With razor saliva, this giant needs just one bite.
Bacteria finish you off in one clot. Doesn't matter

how fast you get away, they smell for miles. Imagine
their discoverers, how remote the islands, beaches, water,

then falling asleep—in the morning, all that's left
is a bloody shoe, pair of glasses, and a few survivors'

bad stories. *Here be dragons*, first explorers scrawled
on maps. Milton said, *solitude is sometimes best society*.

How wrong with these cannibals, who rule with no
competition. In ancient times, dragons shared

land with a dwarf race of people with grapefruit
sized heads. Skeletons of each were found in caves.

Who hunted whom? In island rule, if you want
something, wait for it. Swallow it whole—the hide,

hooves, the tourist. Isolate and grow large.
If devoured, emerge as skeleton, bone dressed

in the finest suit—a coat out of the ribs, the sternum
playing a tie; the clavicle, a collar.

The Night Watch

I hunt in the mirror for a scare
inside my mouth, the first white
spot on the back of my throat, checking
if my gums have receded from the teeth
in high arches, for tenderness
in the neck, armpits and groin,
a colorful blotch on the back of my thigh,
on my feet, between the toes. The lint
from a black sock shocks me.

I am six, finishing a nightly bath.
I do not unplug the drain. I decide
to bob face down on the water,
to fake I am drowning.
I dip my head under, closing my eyes,
turning my head to the side. I float;
my breath makes dents in the water.
I wait for my father to come up the stairs.

Says Narcissus to the Mirror

Call me stud, stallion—
I'll tell you what it's like to be

desired, everything met
with *yes*. When you lie

with man's emotions, he
gives you things. My body—

a death machine, I've demons
under the bed, destroyer

personality taken over.
I want you to come

with me now, quiet
as magma. Do you need

to be alone, have you punched
a wall, smiled at the camera?

Please unhinge the limiter,
your mouth, turn the flowers

to stone. I'm the child
you've been given, reborn

in paradise, burning chariot in head.
This is a madness of two where I drink myself.

Scary Movie Marathon
The Silence of the Lambs

My argument: a Rose Kennedy cocktail
is named a Rose Kennedy because

*Rosemary had a lobotomy. The straw
being the icepick that swirls the cranberry*

 pink as our drinks. My date
is a murderer. His art

is to sew patterns based
on Barbie's wild proportions.

He shows his models off
in boxes for show. I see

the senator's daughter
in the pit of lotion, a tune

playing goodbye
to horses. In Nevada,

the wild horses are salt
in death's head.

I'm running away.
Early morning, mowing

the lawn. Something high-pitched
from beneath the blade.

The rabbits were screaming
as they were beheaded

through the grass. A sinking
feeling into the coils,

heavy as a trinket
in the esophagus. A moth

dances above me.
I'm in his overcoat.

Mother

Madonna of material, I snapped
my rosary, made it into a bracelet for you
at Sunday school, sneaked downstairs
to see you lit before inflamed crosses,
my fingers scented with your patchouli-
cassette. I get drunk, Madonna.
So drunk I sneak leftover drinks
from the bar. I lose myself in the mirror
plucking gray hairs, tug at the sag
in my belly. I want to conquer my fear of
heights, Madonna. Of having roaches or the virus
inside my body. I want a cheap twenty-two-year-old lover that doesn't
    speak
English. I want my hair bleach blond.
I want to go to the bar, Mother. I want
a vodka double, Mother, a double vodka
Madonna on the rocks.

Skintight

My father hands me gifts he bought Christmas Eve:
an extra-large broadcloth and thirty-four-waist khakis.

I dress different from the boys at school. My shirts fall
at my navel; my jeans are skintight.
I am to wear the outfit or my clothes will be ripped apart—

the neighbors are talking. No deals, no exceptions.
We are all there: my mother, my sister on the couch, my father
urging, *Put them on. Put them on.*

I strip in the bathroom with my back to the mirror.
The shirt hangs to my knees, the pants slide on buttoned.
My face is hollow. My skin—deaf, as the audience,

the family await me outside, my mother knocking,
Put them on for your father.

When I step out my mother will be silent. My sister—gone.
My father will clap his hands. He will look me in the eye, ask me:

Do you feel like a man?

Another Exploitation in Which
I Glamorize the Murder of
JonBenét Ramsey, a Child of Six

JonBenét was a bitch. That's awful—but what the books say.
She was bossy. If she didn't want to do the pageant, that was
that. No one could make her. *C'est tout*—she spoke French.
She was mischievous—police thought enough to lure her killer
into the basement in a game of hide-and-seek. She'd ruin
the landscaper's work. She'd throw tantrums about clothes, pout
she wasn't pretty. She had an effect on people: a murmur
through the room—she was really cooking. Most important
she wanted to win. She'd even compete all over again for a crown
she already won. Therefore, she brought it upon herself. Mom,
former Miss West Virginia, snapped in the mirror and wrangled her.
Daddy used her to get his rocks off. Brother was the jealous little
psychopath. Or the sexual sadist was obsessed. The police wanted sex.
That was semen on her thighs, pubic hair in her sheets, dictionary
found opened to *incest*. The ligature around her neck was erotic
asphyxiation. Sex is what makes all of it work. The magic's
in the makeup of the cord wound around her neck and hands,
above her crown, all under a Christmas tree, mom wailing
for Lazarus to please rise little Miss Colorado to accuse
no one. Choose your motive—Ramseys did it, intruder did it. It's
easy to pull the garrotte tighter forgetting she's already
dead. The whodunit kidnapped her under cover of the tabloid
fantasy network. Once she asked, *Do roses know they have thorns*?
Let's not lie to her.

* * *

Patsy, Patsy, Patsy—the lead detective was obsessed with Patsy.
Patsy and the role of pageants. Patsy beating cancer with the power
of money. Patsy wearing fur. Patsy never wearing an outfit
twice. Patsy with the Amex card swiped with no abandon—
quicksilver calligraphy, a style change at her command, her pad—
her paper—her felt tipped pen—pages torn—the start of a practice
ransom note. Dear Mrs. Ramsey peering through splayed fingers, glued
to the officers, the couch when the body of JonBenét was rushed
up the stairs. Patsy chaining cigarettes between interrogations. Patsy
needing specific clothes from the house, those black jeans—the fiber
evidence that must've been there. Patsy was a liar, Patsy knew that murder
is what it seems, that she would never want to step foot in that house
again. *Torch* it, she said. In the theory of prosecution—this was a rage
    attack
centered around bedwetting. It was constant. JonBenét did it every day.
The bruising on her neck was consistent with the twisting of the collar,
the knuckles against her throat as Patsy spiraled out of control, cracking
her skull against the tub, whisking her down the stairs through garland
that caught in her hair, round and round her neck with the ligature
in the wine cellar—all staging down to her twenty-two minute devolution
as the author of ransom note. Patsy covered her with a blanket, changed
the underwear, drew the heart on her palm, applied the duct tape, corded
the hands above her head, all done preciously in time for the panic
later that morning. Months before, she scolded JonBenét for wearing
a jacket in a restaurant because she was cold. Patsy took it off,
    reminded her:
You're still on show.

*   *   *

I did not kill JonBenét, *I did not have anything*
to do with it. I loved that child with my whole
of my heart and soul.

JonBenét did not have anything to do
with my heart, my soul. JonBenét loved

heart, soul, and did not have anything. Kill
my heart with my child and do with it anything
not whole. My child

did have heart and I loved anything with soul. Do not kill
anything whole. I have JonBenét with my heart.

That whole child did have my heart, I did not kill
my soul that I loved.

With JonBenét, kill soul and anything whole.

That child, my heart loved. I did not do that
to my child. I did that to my child.

*   *   *

John was just as guilty in their eyes. John, the business man money bags
calling lawyers two hours after the discovery of the body, John
pointing the finger at friends. John wandering around the house, hidden
from the first responder's eye for hours checking mail, pacing,

booking a flight to Atlanta. John making a bee-line for the basement,
screaming *Oh my god* opening the wine cellar. It was John leaning over
the body, asking *Is she dead?* John placing everyone in the coat of the law.
In a theory, John was caught red-handed by a screaming Patsy who
      swung—
connected to JonBenét. But for a reason, the police turned away. John
suffered from the death of another child, another marriage. John would
be protective—John wouldn't let this happen. John knew about death.

Was stoic; Patsy hysterical. John was the armor here; but he knew.
The troubling thing is the first responder looks into his eyes
that morning, JonBenét beneath them. She counts her bullets. Liar
liar John with his pants on fire.

*　*　*

*To those of you who may want to ask, let me address very directly, I did not kill
my daughter, JonBenét. There have also been innuendoes that she has been or was
sexually molested. I can tell you those were the most hurtful innuendoes to us as a
family. They are totally false. JonBenét and I had a very close relationship, I will
miss her dearly for the rest of my life.*

There are those that want totally hurtful innuendoes
that I sexually did that to my daughter. I do not have

a family. Most relationships have been hurtful, I do not want
a family molested. Did you have a hurtful family?

Most relationships are false—total innuendoes
that may want to address my hurt, to kill directly. I want

innuendoes for my daughter. You are hurtful, directly false, close
to killing my family. JonBenét, life may directly want you.

Can you rest? Did you ask for a false family?
Address those close to you. They are the most harmful.

                    ✻   ✻   ✻

Burke played with a toy that night and then went to bed. Slept **47**
through the whole of it. The parents claimed he knew nothing—
whisked him away hours before the display of the body. That's not
his voice on the tail of the 911 call. That's not John saying *We're not
talking to you.* He said he just heard Mom going psycho, had a desire
to see what's going on, but stayed afraid. Excited, relieved was how
he described on seeing his parents reunited until they conveyed: JonBenét
was in heaven. In the interviews with child psychologists, Burke plays
Guess Who? He knocks a suspect down incorrectly, exclaims *You're
not dead yet.* How hard have you hit a sibling? Have you accidently
pushed too hard? Hit too hard? Wound them into an emergency room?
The second lead detective accused Burke of growing sibling
resentment—leading to murder. Burke defecated in her bed, smeared
shit on her presents. He rocked her cheek with a golf club to the point
    that
Patsy brought her to a plastic surgeon. He was intimate with knots
from boy scouts, could've tied the cord on the paintbrush. He knew
that JonBenét was hit on the head before those details leaked. Jealous
brother releases the pent-up frustration of attention spent on beauty
queen sister, all those hour-long lessons, costumes, trophies, he grabs
the flashlight, the game of doctor ends, the cord snaps. Burke draws
a family portrait for the psychologist. JonBenét isn't there. *She died.*

* * *

This is a case about opposites. The younger the child
found dead in the house, the more likely

it's the parents, someone related. The guilty
will do everything in their might not to find

the body. But here we have John with the discovery,
a wait for the ransom spent without

a single mention of Why doesn't anyone check the basement?
The accused often get the show

on the road. JonBenét was found
torso wrapped in a blanket, arms, feet sticking out—

not the usual loving given to the hermetic
seal of staging where everything

is about care. Mothers
don't just bash their child's head in, coil

their neck to a furrow, then pen a three-page
ransom note. Or do they?

Do the parents—no history of abuse or scandal
all of a sudden turn police trickster sociopath mastermind

over Christmas night, seemingly growing closer over the years
when others divorce? At this point, are they beyond

the umbrella of suspicion? A lie
is fine, so nod yes.

* * *

Santa did it. A pedophile did it. The parents rendered assistance to   **49**
   someone
who did it. Housekeeper did it. Neighbor did it. Disgruntled coworker
did it. Look at JonBenét. She was an investment. One hundred eighteen
thousand reasons to crack through the window in the basement, write
the War & Peace of ransom notes, sample each room in the mansion,
   turnaround—
you're lost— then start the day after Christmas with a stun gun
to the cheek, goodnight. The intruder does his thing then places the note,
good morning. Fake news abound: there was snow on the ground, no
footprints, all of the doors, windows locked. The Ramseys lost track
of all of the keys given out—all those housekeepers, gardeners, workers.
The house is a suspect itself. John took a melatonin that night, Patsy said
she went to bed. A scream rings at midnight that a neighbor hears. All
asleep, the sound absorbed by the house. The intruder was profiled to be
criminally unsophisticated, using items around him, the time spent inside
not unheard of. The police hid news of the saliva found on her panties
for months, the unknown match also under her fingernails. Someone
had a ticket for JonBenét. Before the murder, the parents found unknown
objects in their summer home. Someone had been sleeping in her bed.
Someone stole candy cane decorations from the front yard a week after

the murder. Someone stood in the alleyway behind the house with stick and cord, *You can't have her, she's mine.* And the same guy at the funeral, stating *Don't you just want to strangle her?* A house sitter disappeared from across the alley within days of the discovery of the body. Someone pulled the blanket over our eyes.

*   *   *

50   New year, new issue of the Globe, catch six autopsy photos—
the dead hands of the six-year-old, the murder weapon—all leaked

to the Globe. The earth moves beneath her feet, through headlines—
Little Beauty Sex Murder—artist's renditions, her body sprawled across

every detail of the autopsy report. JonBenét is the little girl
that lives in the aisle, dies at checkout. *I want to be*

a cowboy sweetheart, she sings over Japanese TV. She does the dance
she does so well for the checkbook journalism, she gives

the sensational photographs, headlines we want. She is everyone's
daughter, spiraling through the Enquirer

in various stages of undress: killed
in her parent's bed, the desperate fight, daddy did it,

mom's secret bombshell confession, the rape shocker grim
truth that reveals vital evidence. Focus on the family

ghost. How did she get that bruise? Where did she get
that spot? Lighten the load, toss the paper in the cart. JonBenét feels

the wind on her face. The sun sets in the West. She's
not your daughter.

*   *   *

Tighten the garrote till she can't

breathe. Tighten the tabloid. Tighten
the television. Tighten the documentary
with dead JonBenét as narrator. Tighten
the child actor. Tighten the flashlight
demonstrations on a watermelon to signify
a six year old's skull. Tighten the anniversary
plastered all over the media. Tighten the trial
by public by the public. Tighten the autopsy photos
leaked to the press to your policy of privacy. Tighten
it again because you like it, because you flipped
at the supermarket, because you clicked. Tighten
the theories. Tighten them till you're inside her room, till
you're both the beauty and the beast. Tighten them till you're
en route to the basement, unlatching the wine cellar door. Tighten them
till the exploration of this exploitation wounds excitement to hit
empty inside. Tighten them around your presumed innocence. You're
only interested. She's only dead. Keep tightening till her little head
pops off. Keep tightening because it's not enough. Keep tightening
because it will never be enough. Tighten it because breathing
is natural. Tighten it because her chest will continue to rise,

fall as the headlines cycle one hundred eighteen thousand times. Tighten it to keep the conjuring going. Tighten it to revive Little Miss Christmas. Tighten it to draw another heart on her palm. Tighten it to try to make it stop. Tighten it to solve it. It's out there somewhere. Tighten it because breathing isn't real.

Gun Porno

A shot in my ass, four pills back,
I've never wanted a gun so bad—
a gun in my hands,

your gun, my gun, transgression,
clack clack clack—this is fun,
holding my breath

till I pass out, my first
taste of blood, thirteen, a gun
pointed at me, one single shot

rang through the house, the magic
of murder ringing, singing,
calling out your name.

I'm building a mansion
where doors open
to solid walls; with my gun

I sleep in a different
room each night
or I'll die. I want

to be tougher, spit
in my eye, throw my arm
to a corner, sit spin stop

the ride. I'll have staircases
to nowhere, decoy
rooms, a roulette parlor

where I speak with the dead.
Who's next? I'll catch
love with a gun, play alone

with guns, my gun, your gun, a gun
to give me life, a gun
to stop the rise.

If I Did It

A lover's quarrel, fatal attraction, deadly lust—
all of the generic headlines above, my face
plastered. He's dead. What a disaster. Now
that's out of the way, what the hell happened?
For the answer, look to the photos. Happy times.
The sentimental music plays. All signs
pointed to that I was happy. Maybe I was
in love. You'd hear my friends, family speak:
not everything was what it seemed. After
commercials, things fade darker—a game,
truth-or-dare out of control. The blindfold,
the restraints. Maybe I was chained. Certainly
my behavior was odd, not afraid
to be in the tabloid. *Surely I get pleasure*
from confessing. Living, I tell the press.
I boil down to a few sound bites. If
I did it, I must be a wonderful liar, victim
in carnage, opening the door to police
in a white robe, yoga while interrogated. If
guilty, I'm a monster. But the facts are
irrelevant, staging upon staging, inconvenient
truth. I only need to sway one, just need
you to hang it or walk. I'm a mind hunter
on the trail to our connection. I know
I can convince you.

Prayer

What a sweet tablet I slip under
the tongue this Sunday, walk

through the ginkgo fruit all vomit-inducing,
homeless asking for cents to catch that magic

bus that's always leaving somewhere.
Miss L.A. is buying lollipops

at the liquor store with dimes because she likes
to sleep with something in her mouth.

I have nothing to say
about the hyper anorexic

serving my Bloody Mary. I've ripped
my nail off and I've slept

with every man in my neighborhood.
This is what you wanted, an encounter with

being pushed to the absolute limit.
Tomorrow is my birthday. I'm going

to escape to the crystal city, an inner
world where light ends the horizon,

violence is inaccessible. I'm
in the same building I've always been in,

the abandoned one next door,
traffickers inside the rooms. I lose myself to horror.

Honey Bee

Never mind the wasp—
ball it inside a fist
until the temperature
immolates to lethal.

Or the spider—
in an attack, leave
yourself inside, stinger
detached, death in minutes.

I was standing, knees
bent, hand over hand
on the driver, my eye
on a dandelion head.

I had beheaded a dozen
that day, their faces
littered the back yard.

The swarm came
from the porch,
a black funnel of bees
inhaling grass, then my

eyes, my shirt. At this
moment, I want to lie
out of need for crisis,
to say I was stung,
my throat swelled,
the taste of metal
in my mouth.

Tick

Pick one of the doors in the hallway.
Open it, lock yourself inside. Exhaust
all items in the room. Cram them

in your heart's lock box. Eat every
crumb. Put your feet on the furniture.
Hitch a ride. Pass for a deadbeat.

May. My mother warns they emerge.
Afternoons, my sister and I survey
our hair, legs, skin we cannot see.

When she strikes the match,
I'm on the mud room floor—shorts
rolled, with a black tab—too deep

to pull out behind my knee. The tick
rushes, eight legs disappear into skin.
I prepare for bull's-eye mornings,

wear pants all summer long. Those
checks where I combed over my body
in witch hunt, undressing

to spot the mark of parasite, where
if finding nothing meant it must
be buried inside, that health

is a sleeve,
an outfit placed on daily
panic, nudity—a great deal of it.

Virgin

I am afraid to go into my room. She
is there after school, tidying, folding
my shirts—room spotless. She
asks *Why do you want to get sick?*

Why do you want filth in your mouth?
I'm a virgin and believe AIDS
hides inside the spinal cord. If
I have sex with a man, one day
it will release, a sort of magic. She
leaves an internet printout under
my pillow, a story of recovery
from a college boy. *This is normal.*
This is a phase.

When we fuck, I think too much
of the fire beneath sheets she
planted—the dirt on my palms
I can't scour, that constant rise
of skin when you pass through me,
faster than the wild flowers
flying by down the long stretch
of highway—all Black-eyed
Susans, periwinkles, the perfume.

Scary Movie Marathon
Friday the 13th

Maybe it was short-shorts Kevin Bacon
half-naked, arrow through the throat,
the danger of Camp Crystal Lake where sex
equals death, that taught me how to find
Ryan's cock in my basement
in the eighth grade, my hand
inching across the couch
to his gym shorts. Maybe it was
that he was moving to Aurora—
that stroking him in the darkness
could keep him. That night
my mother almost walked in.
What are you boys doing? she yelled
from the top of the stairs. That night
we slept in separate rooms.
He left silent in the morning. We hugged
in my driveway, my eyes bloodshot
from watching my door all night.

Ars Poetica

How devil-may-care this wolf spider bite
moves to the elbow outward in the illuminated

night. I'm barefoot on slate pulling a string
out of my mouth to make bones dance. There

is no end—nothing comes out but poison I
stitch through myself, raveling poison until

pure. Watch me do this alone, watch me
take this poison daily, a diet of roots, berry

stains scrubbed over myself in salt and more
poison. Ring the bell—I'm on a pilgrimage to life

or to love—though that isn't novel either,
a Russian said. Look—I'm a fairy tale, the old

man trapped in the house all fed, lacquered.
I've no life but the words keep coming out my mouth.

Talking to the Colossus

On one hand I've counted
how many times I've gone
to where I'm meant to be lost:
in the line of your calm brood, face
without eyes. To make you vocal.
How can I sink into your faults? Listen:
it's the apocalypse. *Hare hare Krishna—*
I'm joining a cult to float through it.
There will be a bed I tuck
myself into, I'll tie the knots on my shoes.
I'll bask in mourning,
I'm a popular tourist site, a machine
with a trick. Watch as I climb your leg.
You're out there somewhere irretrievable.
Such luck. We will watch the shore
come in together, apart. At sunrise
I'm going to the top of the world.

The Twelve Hours of the Night

Tonight you are not the expert of your body.
Become comfortable with separation, your eyes

masked, the desire to live germinating
out of the inexhaustible bloom of your mouth.

Tonight, a serpent cleaves down both veils
of your body efficiently as scarab, faster

than shadow. Below the spoon-fed moon,
seven mosquitoes tread on your tongue

weighted with names you must recite, all
unknown. Remember

what you have not done,
what you have not stolen.

You must kneel down in this terrible place.
You must place your flesh into a tabernacle,

embrace snake. Remember
so far back you consume yourself.

The inner work you've done—oblivion.
Opposition is always there, a bird of prey

moving this boat of your life by a feather.
Write this poem when the last hour winds

itself asleep at the threshold of transformation.
Send forth your words. Stand as voice.

Everything out of your mouth is a lie.

In Seconds

Second story on the news: second
story rapist strikes through fire escapes—

The lesbian couple above me swear
they hear footsteps on metal at night,

tape a police sketch of the man
outside their window, install bars

after a knife-point victim is held
a street away. Around the world

people report visitations of a shadow
man of smokeless flame

in corners of the room
observing. I stopped dead to check

my pulse on the sidewalk today,
near an alley where a homeless

man now stands silent, shirtless
leaning against a staff for hours.

I understand nothing at night,
dream of peeling my feet ankle

to toe, waiting days on the bed
until they freshen and awake heart

in mouth to think how we prowl—
live only blocks removed, yet we deny

comfort—the inner malady
being forced out.

Apollo

A final splash of the dew and a slip
        of pollen on the tongue,
I am drought coming to reap

what prospers away from me—
your eyes. On the threshing
        floor I will make the separation

first at the crown, the flesh above
        as below in coils as the need
        to depollute your body flows

without hesitation from the fingers
        to the breast, the notes I'm playing
        on the ribs hysteric, livid. Raised

        by wolves, never apologize
for the want of flesh, the politics
        of pelt. No animals howl

at the moon—a myth of jackals,
        and ecstasy makes no sound
        during the death of a hundred slow

cuts. In between every change,
I love every part of you as I go
      deeper, the complete skin falls

to the river, on the shore where
      you stand suffered, transfigured—
the stranger inside you.

Safe Danger

The city is burning, but this is not a drought.
I'm wandering the mezzanine, night stalker
in bloom. Watch out for the glass—I'm out
with the slosh

purpose to build a lust excitement up
to toss my shoes from the bridge & I can't

come down. Go out blind,
forget it all.
At the scene of the crime—
there's no fence, the door unlocked. If I lived here
I'd be home now. I tighten the bind
till I see the light capturing myself. Here we are again—
in my delights, night. Break
my finger; slash hand, spoil
shirt—red anyways. What else
does one do at night? Things make sense
but they're not real. Night lulls.
I write an inmate. That's safe danger—

when the murderer writes your name.
Talking to the serial killer, I flirt. Show me

how to do it, the love poetry, the hand trace hello
in my mailbox from the land of plenty. Ask me

for money, tell me about the guy who got beaten
to death in the yard, put me under

the pillow—I'm your prison
pin-up boy.

I juggle the switchblade inside my bedside table,
baseball bat behind the door, check the doors,

closets. There are no witnesses to this stalking
through the night. I haven't revealed anything

just yet. Maybe I say things so much they're just
vapor. Maybe so. This ransom note is longer

than three lines. We have him. He's
alive—happiness for only a million dollars.

I sit here all night wrapped up in a bow.

ACKNOWLEDGEMENTS

Thanks to the editors of the following publications in which many of these poems first appeared, some in slightly different form:

Assaracus: "Komodo Dragon," "In Seconds," "Marsyas," "Mosquito," "Ritual," "Tick," "Virgin"

Bloom: "The Night Watch," "Siberia"

Chelsea Station: "How To Begin"

Glitterwolf: "Scary Movie Marathon: The Amityville Horror," "Scary Movie Marathon: The Silence of the Lambs"

Kettle Blue Review: "Hymn to Isis," "On the Casting Couch"

Knockout: "After It Rains"

Lambda Literary: "Anne Sexton's Last Drink," "Lindsay Lohan"

MiPOesias: "The Bathed One," "Inside"

Poet Lore: "True Crime"

Prairie Schooner: "Mother"

Quarterly West: "Says Narcissus to the Mirror"

Seltzer: "Cobra," "Honey Bee," "The Twelve Hours of the Night"

Toe Good Poetry: "Gay Fiction"

West Branch: "Apollo," "Diet of the Saints"

"After It Rains" received first runner-up for *Knockout's* 2012 International Memorial Reginald Shepherd Poetry Prize.

"Anne Sexton's Last Drink" and "Lindsay Lohan" were featured on Lambda Literary's Poetry Spotlight (www.LambdaLiterary.org).

"Gun Porno" was featured as poem of the day for the HIV Here & Now Project.

"Skintight" was featured as poem of the week at SplitThisRock.org.

"True Crime" was the winner of the 2017 Enoch Pratt Library Poetry Contest.

The following poems appeared in the collection *Caligula's Playhouse* (Mason Jar Press, 2016): "Marsyas," "Inside," "Gay Fiction," "Siberia," "The Bathed One," "Lindsay Lohan," "Diet of the Saints," "Anne Sexton's Last Drink," "Cobra," "How to Begin," "After It Rains," "On the Casting Couch," "Mosquito," "The Night Watch," "Says Narcissus to the Mirror," "Ritual," "Love Song," "Mother," "Skintight," "Prayer," "Honey Bee," "Virgin," Ars Poetica," "Tick," "The Twelve Hours of the Night," In Seconds," "Apollo."

Thanks to the many people who lent valuable feedback and support: David Keplinger, Kyle Dargan, Barbara Goldberg, David Bergman, Matthew Bushman, Jenny Dunnington, Chet'la Sebree, Jenna Ogilvie, Will Byrne, Carolyn White, Madonna, Carolyn Clarke, and Mason Jar Press. Without their help and support, this book would not have been written.

STEPHEN ZERANCE's poems have appeared in *West Branch*, *Prairie Schooner*, *Quarterly West*, *Assaracus*, and *Knockout*, among others. He has also been featured on the websites of Lambda Literary and Split This Rock. He received his MFA from American University, where he received the Myra Sklarew award. Stephen lives in Baltimore, Maryland with an extensive shoe collection. Find him on twitter: @stephnz, or on instagram: @stephenzerance @lvcifers_revenge.

INDOLENT BOOKS Indolent Books is a small nonprofit poetry press founded in 2015 and operating in Brooklyn, N.Y. Indolent publishes poetry by underrepresented voices whose work is innovative, provocative, and risky, and that uses all the resources of poetry to address urgent racial, social, and economic justice concerns.

CPSIA information can be obtained
at www.ICGtesting.com
Printed in the USA
FSHW04n0450200418
47020FS